BUSINESS
start-up
HANDBOOK

BUSINESS *start-up* HANDBOOK

Guidelines & Pitfalls

Peter C. Sundt

Cibolo Press

Houston, Texas

Published by:
Cibolo Press
230 Arborway
Houston, Texas 77057
713-780-4401

ISBN: 0-9668547-1-3

PRINTED IN THE UNITED STATES OF AMERICA

Book Production: Phelps & Associates

Cataloging in Publication Data
(prepared by Quality Books)

Sundt, Peter C.
        Business start-up handbook : guidelines and
    pitfalls / Peter C. Sundt.
        p. cm.
        LCCN: 98-74584
        ISBN: 0-9668547-1-3

        1. New business enterprises--Management.
    2. Entrepreneurship. 3. Success in business.
    I. Title

    HD62.5.S48 1998   658.4'21
                                    QBI98-1541

Table of Contents

Chapter 4:
Choosing a Name

Chapter 5:
Raising the Money

Chapter 6:
Running Lean and Mean

Chapter 7:
Keeping the Books

Chapter 8:
Financial Controls

Chapter 9:
Managing Cash

Chapter 10:
Insurance—A Necessary Burden

Chapter 11:
Marketing

Foreword

This book is aimed at all those aspiring entrepreneurs who yearn to start their own business and be their own boss. There is no doubt that owning and running one's own business can be most satisfying ... and very often monetarily rewarding. Unfortunately, however, the grim statistics indicate that a depressingly large percentage of business start-ups fail in the first year or two. There are many factors that together determine the success or failure of a new enterprise. The following pages offer some suggested guidelines to follow and pitfalls to avoid in the quest for business success.

Chapter 1:

The Idea—Will it Fly?

Too many businesses—started with an idea that won't fly—find failure almost a certainty. Whether the idea involves a product or a service, each entreprenuer must carefully study the market and the competition before ordering business cards and estimating profit.

Surveying the Marketplace

The first step to take after making the decision to start your own business is to consult all printed matter available that pertains to the type of business you are contemplating. This would include trade journals, catalogs and industry registers (all found at the public library). *The Thomas Register of Industrial Products and Services* is a very valuable reference. The yellow pages should be consulted too, especially if the new business will serve mainly the local market. Also, a few hours spent on the Internet exploring the web pages of potential competitors will reveal a lot about the state-of-the-art and competition in a chosen field. **Remember, many "bright" ideas fade in the light of what's already out there.**

Search for competitor information on the Internet with these directories:
* American Export Register: www.aernet.com/English
* BizWeb: www.bizweb.com
* InfoSpace: www.infospace.com
* BigBook: www.bigbook.com
* Europages: www.europages.com/home-en.html
* Harris Info Sources: www.harrisinfo.com (American manufacturers)

Canvassing Potential Customers

Most businesses are started with the intention of selling a product or service to others. Accordingly, it makes sense to identify potential customers and ask them what they think of your business idea. Canvass as many potential customers as possible in order to arrive at some sort of consensus, since the opinion of a single prospective customer can often be misleading. If the proposed idea meets with a lukewarm reception, the prudent entrepreneur should seriously consider going back to the drawing board. **All too often, ideas are pursued without testing customer acceptance—with predictably disappointing results.**

Additional Internet directories:
- Thomas Register of American Manufacters: www.thomasregister.com
- SEC Database: www.sec.gov/edgarhp.html
- www.companiesonline.com
- www.555-1212.com

Additional references on the Internet:
- U.S. Department of Commerce sites: www.doc.gov (main site); www.stat-usa.gov (Internet Info System); www.bea.doc.gov (Bureau of Economic Analysis)

Defining the need for your business:
Identify the competition.
Canvass potential customers through telephone, mail, and Internet surveys.

Additional references:

- *Encyclopedia of Associations*, Gale Research Company
- *National Trade & Professional Associations of the U.S.*,
    Columbia Books, Inc. (202) 898-0662
- *Encyclopedia of Business Information Sources*, Gale Research Company
- U.S. Chamber of Commerce (202) 659-6000
- Business ratio studies and cost of doing business studies,
    Dun & Bradstreet (908) 508-7600 and
    National Cash Register Company (937) 445-5000
- Standard & Poor's *Register of Corporations, Directors & Executives*
- *Where to Find Business Information*, John Wiley & Sons Publishers
- *The Thomas Register of American Manufacturers*,
    Thomas Publishing Co.
- Industry Analysts: contact the U.S. Department of Commerce
- Company Case Studies from the *Directory of Harvard Business School Cases and Related Course Material* (617) 495-6117
- *Almanac of Consumer Markets*,
    American Demographics (800) 828-1133
- International Franchise Association Membership Directory
- The Information Catalog (bimonthly)
    FIND/SVP (800) 346-3787 NY: (212) 645-4500
- U.S. Industrial Outlook, Superintendent of Documents

Checking Out the Competition

Unless your proposed product or service is truly unique, there will be existing competition. Furthermore, if the total market is not rapidly growing, your own business revenues will have to come out of the hides of your competitors. **A thorough research of the competition's products or services and their pricing structure is imperative.** Research includes obtaining competitive literature and price lists, scanning trade journals, reviewing websites and attending trade shows where competitors may be exhibiting. Also, finding out how the competition is rated in the eyes of potential customers is worth the effort. (This information can be obtained when you canvass potential customers.)

With the possible exception of commodities, a business based solely on offering lower prices is not very promising. There is an old saying that goes, "When introducing a new product or service against entrenched competition, one must offer at least two advantages—one of which can be price."

Is the New Product
Idea Really New?

If the business is based on a novel product idea, one is well advised to refer to U.S. Patent Office records for prior inventions involving the same idea. This can be done by hiring a patent attorney to conduct a patent search. Alternatively, abstracts of most U.S. patents can be accessed on the Internet websites of patent search services, such as Dun & Bradstreet and IBM. Hard copies of existing patents can be ordered online from the same services or from the U.S. Patent office in Washington, DC.

Additional references:
- Dun & Bradstreet: www.aol.telebase.com/mpatents
- IBM Patent Server: www.patents.ibm.com
- Obtain a Directory of Manufacturing Companies from your state Chamber of Commerce or Department of Economic Development.
- Division of Corporations' (in each state) list of newly-formed companies
- Look in your local yellow pages phone book.
- U.S. Patent Office: www.uspto.gov (800) 786-9199
- Patent search company: there are many patent search companies on the internet. Simply enter "patent" in any major search engine (Yahoo, InfoSeek, Lycos, Excite, AOL, etc.) to conduct a search
- Consumer Price Indexes on the Internet: www.stats.bls.gov/ciphome.html

---

The Author's Own Experience

I must confess that I didn't follow the above guide-lines when I started my business. Instead, I began with the idea of contract engineering for a living, while keeping an eye out for an opportunity to pursue. It almost didn't work. The consulting business was not profitable, and only by sheer luck an opportunity presented itself before the seed money ran out.

SCORE:

• The Service Corps of Retired Executives offers a wealth of information and support for entrepreneurs. They have volunteers throughout the country, ready to offer guidance and practical input. (800) 634-0245 or on the Internet at: www.score.org

(They also offer free Email counseling.)

Chapter 2:

The Business Plan

Why a Business Plan?

The best way to anticipate the future of a new business is to develop a written business plan, which sets out the ideas and goals of the entrepreneur and the steps to achieve them. **This is absolutely necessary if capital is to be raised from lenders or from the sale of stock.** Even if the entrepreneur can finance the start-up without outside help, a business plan is essential in establishing the feasibility of the business, assessing the capital required and estimating the time lapse before profits might begin. Do not neglect this important step.

Business plan checklist:
- an Operations Forecast
- a description of the company and the principals/founders
- an explanation of the market for the product or service
- what makes your product or service unique?
- a Marketing Plan:
- prices and how they compare with competitors
- design and development costs and a timetable
- manufacturing (if applicable) and Operations Plan
- 3 years of P&L and cash flow projections
- estimated balance sheets at start, six-months and annually for 3 years
- a Management Plan (how the company will be organized and what constitutes the management team)
- schedule of all business activity
- what difficulties might arise and how they will be handled.

Writing a Business Plan

A written business plan will force the entrepreneur to confront the many tasks and questions that must be addressed. It provides potential lenders, investors and associates the information they need to evaluate your business prospects. The business plan should include:

- an explanation of the potential market,
- a description of the proposed product or service vis-a-vis the competition,
- an estimate of the time to develop the proposed business, including promotion and field testing,
- an estimate of the capital required to launch the business (see "Operations Forecast"),
- the proposed method for raising the required capital (see "Raising the Money"),
- an estimate of the required initial staffing,
- a long range forecast showing the anticipated profits once the business is off the ground—which is what potential investors are most interested in.

Preparing an Operations Forecast

An Operations Forecast is simply a spreadsheet that shows predicted revenues, costs and resulting profit or loss in successive time intervals after starting a business. **It is a very important step in the business plan, as it gives the entrepreneur and potential investors an idea of the capital required to launch the business and the time line when profits can be expected.** A typical Operations Forecast is shown in Figure 1. In this hypothetical example no revenues are expected in the first three months, as it will take at least that long to develop the product or service and to stimulate the first sale. After that, sales are seen to rise gradually, so that after one year the business is finally breaking even. However, up to that time the hypothetical business has been losing money each month. The accumulated loss at the end of the year is seen to be $80,000 and expenditures on capital equipment have totaled $50,000.

Add a couple of months of working capital for good measure, and the estimated initial capital required comes to:

Accumulated operating loss ....$ 80,000
Capital equipment expenditures 50,000
Additional working capital required.............. 70,000
TOTAL $200,000

The numbers will, of course, vary widely depending upon the type and size of the business. When preparing an Operations Forecast, one should try to be very conservative in one's estimates regarding revenues, costs and delays. Usually, the entrepreneur's most conservative estimates turn out to be too optimistic. **The important thing to remember is that if insufficient capital is raised in the beginning, additional capital will be much harder to come by after the initial capital is exhausted.**

Note: Have your business plan reviewed by an accountant, attorney, SCORE volunteer, or other qualified professionals; then carefully consider their input.

Figure 1: Operations Forecast

Months after start-up

	1	2	3	4	5	6	7	8	9	10	11	12	Totals
Cash Revenue	0	0	0	4,000	6,000	8,000	10,000	12,000	16,000	20,000	24,000	30,000	130,000
Cost of Sales	0	0	0	2,000	3,000	4,000	5,000	6,000	8,000	10,000	12,000	14,000	64,000
Gross Profit	0	0	0	2,000	3,000	4,000	5,000	6,000	8,000	10,000	12,000	16,000	66,000
Expenses	10,000	10,000	10,000	10,000	11,000	11,000	12,000	12,000	14,000	14,000	16,000	16,000	146,000
Profit (Loss)	(10,000)	(10,000)	(10,000)	(8,000)	(8,000)	(7,000)	(7,000)	(6,000)	(6,000)	(4,000)	(4,000)	0	(80,000)
Capital Equipment	20,000	10,000	10,000	6,000	0	2,000	0	0	2,000	0	0	0	50,000

Chapter 3:

The Business Organization

Sole Proprietorship

This is the very simplest form of organization, involving the least amount of regulations and paperwork. A sole proprietor is his or her own boss, reporting to no one. He or she is the sole owner, the sole provider of capital, the sole beneficiary of gains and the sole sufferer of losses, if any, in the business. **In a sole proprietorship there is no distinction between personal and business debts.** Business income or loss is reported on the sole proprietor's personal income tax return. Many small businesses start as sole proprietorships to keep things simple and later incorporate to avoid personal liability.

Additional References:
- The IRS Publication 334: *Tax Guide for Small Businesses*, explains sole proprietorship, partnership, corporation, and S corporation in further detail.
- IRS on the Internet: www.irs.ustreas.gov/prod
- IRS tax forms on the Internet:
  www.taxweb.com/forms/state_intforms.html

Partnership

When two or more individuals join to operate a business, the entity is called a partnership. **The partners share equally in the assets and liabilities and in the profits or losses.** Although a partnership is a separate business entity, creditors and claimants can look to the partners' personal assets for satisfaction. A partnership files a separate business income tax return; however, the profit or loss is reported on each partner's personal tax return.

The Uniform Partnership Act:

This act defines a partnership as "an association of two or more persons to carry on as co-owners of a business for profit." The written agreement between the partners is known as the "Articles of Partnership." These articles can be recorded by the Clerk of Court in your location.

There are limited and general partnerships. In a limited partnership the limited partner invests money but does not act as a manager in the day-to-day running of the business. Limited partners and general partners vary in their ability to be held liable for business debts.

The Corporation

A corporation is a form of business chartered by the Secretary of State and operating as a separate entity from its owners, the shareholders. **As such, a corporation exists as an individual**, even though it may be owned by many shareholders, whose personal assets are shielded from the debts of the corporation and whose ultimate risk is limited to their investment in the shares of the corporation. A corporation is the most formal of business organizations, having by-laws, a board of directors elected by the shareholders and officers elected by the directors.

Corporations are overseen
by state governments.
The "Articles of Incorporation"
are forwarded to the
Secretary of State for approval.

C Corporation

In a C Corporation, the most common form, the corporation files its own income tax return and pays its own taxes, if any. **The shareholder does not report C Corporation income on his or her personal tax return.** However, any dividends or distributions paid by a C Corporation to its shareholders must be reported on each shareholder's personal tax return. This means that such distributions are taxed twice—first when the profits are taxed at the corporate level and again when the profits are paid out to the shareholders.

Additional Reference:
•*How to Form Your Own Corporation Without a Lawyer for Under $50,* Ted Nicholas (Wilmington, Del.: Enterprise Publishing).

S Corporation

In an S Corporation, which operates more like a partnership—but which retains the limited liability advantage of a C Corporation—profits or losses are reported and paid by the shareholders and not by the corporation. This is particularly advantageous for the shareholders of a start-up. Initial losses, if there are any, can be used to offset the personal taxable income of its shareholders. The rules governing an S Corporation limit the number of shareholders and impose other restrictions, so that large businesses with many shareholders or ones having subsidiaries are not eligible. **In general, for a startup business the S Corporation form of organization is ideal.** Even when an S Corporation becomes profitable, it can make tax free distributions to reimburse its shareholders for the business income taxes they are required to pay.

While C Corporations are taxed twice—an S Corporation is not. It is treated as a partnership at taxtime, and is limited to a specific number of shareholders.

The Author's Own Experience

We elected to organize as an S Corporation in order to allow the shareholders to take the initial losses against their personal incomes. Once the company became profitable, we decided to change to a C Corporation, so that the shareholders would not have to report the corporate profits on their tax returns. Later on, when the top personal tax rate was lowered below the corporate tax rate, we changed back to an S Corporation. The resulting personal tax liability each year was covered by a distribution to the shareholders in the same amount.

Limited Liability Company:

• This new way of legally organizing your business offers another choice. Contact your state's Secretary of State for more information or consult your attorney.

Chapter 4:

Choosing a Name

Name Identification

A new business, by definition, has no initial identity in the marketplace. Therefore, the choice of a name deserves careful consideration. **In general, it is a good idea to include in the name a reference to the type of product or service offered.** For instance, if Mr. Jones is starting a shoe repair business, he could choose Jones Shoe Repair or Acme Shoe Repair, but he should avoid such names as The Jones Co. or Acme Inc., as these don't give a clue as to what the business is. Even such giants as IBM and 3M started out with descriptive names—International Business Machines and Minnesota Mining and Manufacturing, respectively. Only after Mr. Jones has grown his business into a large, diversified and well known enterprise should he consider changing the business name to a trendy acronym, such as JSR Inc. Once a business name has been chosen, several steps must be taken to ensure that the name is not already taken.

Reserving a Name for Local Use

If the business is to be conducted only in the local area, the availability of the desired name can be determined from the DBA (Doing Business As) register at the County Clerk's office. If there is a possibility that the business may eventually be statewide, the name should be cleared through and recorded by the Secretary of State in the state where the business will be domiciled. In fact, this is a necessary step if the business is incorporated.

• Check with your state government to determine if your business name must be registered. Some states require a legal notice placed in local newspapers. Banks may require notice from the state that the name has been registered before allowing a checking account in the business name.

• Along with choosing a business name, take time to define your business image. Write a mission statement. Define your style and then ensure every business component, from the way the phone is answered to stationary and business letters, conforms to this style.

Registering a Name Nationwide

As far as clearing a business name for nation-wide use, **unfortunately there does not exist a national clearinghouse for this purpose**. Nevertheless, there are ways to search for prior use of a desired name. One method is to consult the business phone directories of the major cities nationwide. This task is made much easier by the availability of nationwide phone directories on compact disc. Another useful reference is the "Company Name and Trademark Directory" that forms a volume of the *Thomas Register*, which can be found at the public library. Looking up the desired name in the white pages of the Internet is yet another way.

Additional references:
- Yellow Pages: yellowpages.zip2.com
- White Pages: whitepages.com

Avoiding Trademark Infringement

Whether or not the business will be conducted locally or nationwide, one must avoid infringing someone's registered trademark. This can only be determined by consulting the U.S. Patent Office, Trademark Registration. This can be done by hiring a patent attorney or by contacting any of the patent and trademark search services that can be found on the Internet.

• U.S. Patent Office, Trademark Registration:
• Trademark search services: www.uspto.gov (800) 786-9199

The Author's Own Experience

When I chose the name for my start-up business, I consulted the county DBA register, the Secretary of State and the Thomas Register *list of company names and trademarks. Finding no conflict, I ordered letterheads and business forms emblazoned with the chosen name. After about a year, an attorney for a large multinational corporation informed us that our chosen name infringed the registered trademark of their French subsidiary company, whose trademark had been registered in the USA. As the French subsidiary was not active in the USA, their name and trademark were not revealed in our searches, which did not include the U.S. Patent Office. We were able to prevail against this threat only by showing that our respective businesses differed sufficiently that no trade conflict existed.*

Chapter 5:

Raising the Money

Set the Target High

It is a sad fact that many promising new ventures fail for lack of sufficient starting capital. **In fact, most new businesses fail in the first two years, and the major cause is insufficient capital.** The importance of raising enough money to see a new business through its birth and growing pains cannot be over emphasized. Even though an undercapitalized business may eventually survive through second round financing, this normally means that the founder will lose a good part of his or her equity in the process. Some of the ways to raise the money to start a business are discussed on the following pages.

From One's Own Pocket

Keeping in mind all that has been said about raising sufficient starting capital, **the entrepreneur who can finance a new business from his or her own pocket is in the best position to profit from the success of the business.** The obvious reason is that the profits need not be shared with other partners or shareholders. By the same token, any losses in the business cannot be shared with others either. This way may be too risky if a failure of the business would result in the financial ruin or personal bankruptcy of the founder.

Capital and funding can come from the entrepreneur's own pocket, or from a variety of sources such as:

- private capital companies
- state funding programs
- federal funding programs
- certified development companies
- Small Business Administration programs through banks
- SBA small business loans
- Industrial development grants

Borrowing the Money

Borrowing money to fund a start-up is appealing because in doing so the founder does not have to give up equity in the business. However, obtaining a loan for this purpose is a difficult task. **First of all, the lender (a bank for instance) will require that the borrower pledge assets as collateral for the loan, but a start-up business has few, if any, tangible assets to pledge.** Of course, the founder could pledge his personal assets, but that puts him in the position of financing the business from his own pocket, an approach that has already been discussed. Borrowing money to buy capital equipment needed in the business is certainly possible if the equipment itself is pledged as collateral, although a lender will generally loan only part of the cost of the equipment. Loans for land, buildings or equipment are available for small or minority businesses through some state and federal programs. These sources of financing can be obtained from the local Chamber of Commerce and from the local office of the U.S. Small Business Administration.

Borrowing working capital to fund wages, rent, supplies, utilities and other expenses is practically impossible for a start-up business. Only after a business is well established can it borrow working capital by pledging accounts receivable or inventory—things a new start-up business doesn't have. **The main thing to remember is that any loan will have to be paid back with interest, so the anticipated cash flow from the business will have to be sufficient to cover it.** Debt load can be a real burden for a start-up.

Government publications:
• Focus on the Facts (information sheets from the SBA)
  Includes: "How to Raise Money for a Small Business,"
  "Planning...the Most Important Ingredient," "Know Your
  Market," "How to Price Your Product and Services."

Using Other People's Money

If self-financing is rejected as impossible or too risky, and borrowing the money proves to be impractical, one can attempt to use other people's money by asking outside investors to put up risk capital. It is called risk capital because the investor is putting money at risk with the hope and expectation of sharing in the future profits of the enterprise in the form of dividends and/or stock appreciation. **Unlike a loan, which must be repaid with interest on a certain date, an investment is more like a wager, whereby the investor is betting on the success of the company.** A disadvantage of having outside investors is that they become co-owners of the company in exchange for their risk. How much equity they get for their investment will be discussed later.

The most popular form of organization for outside investment is the corporation, which is defined in the chapter entitled "The Business Organization." When seeking investors it is doubly important that a thorough business plan be prepared, as investors will demand it before committing to invest their hard-earned money—and rightfully so.

To start, send potential investors a three-page summary of your business plan. Then send the entire plan upon request.

Maintaining Control

Part of the business plan will have to show how much of the equity in the proposed corporation is for sale and for how much. This is where it gets tricky if the founder proposes to obtain part of his equity in the form of "founder's equity," for which he makes no monetary contribution. It may be appropriate for the founder to obtain some equity in exchange for his or her intellectual investment (the idea for the business, patents, if any, and time spent in research and promotion). The amount of such equity is a matter of what the market will bear. **If the founder proposes too much founder's equity with no cash investment, other prospective investors may object to the resulting dilution of their equity and refuse to join in.** For example, let's imagine that Mr. Jones wants to start a company, and he has determined from an operations forecast that he will need to raise $500,000 capital. Mr. Jones can only invest $200,000 in the venture, meaning that he will seek another $300,000 from other investors. At the same time, Mr. Jones wants to maintain voting control of the corporation and reckons that he should get some free stock in exchange for being the founder. Accordingly, he proposes the following capitalization of the corporation.

Mr. Jones buys 200,000 shares for $200,000
Mr. Jones is granted 150,000 shares at no cost................0
Investors are offered 300,000 shares for $300,000
Totaling 650,000 shares for................. ....$500,000

In this scenario Mr. Jones obtains 350,000 shares for his $200,000 cash investment, while the outside investors get 300,000 shares for their $300,000 invested. Expressed another way, although Mr. Jones put up only 40% of the cash, he ended up with 53.8% of the shares and maintains voting control of the corporation.

In some cases, where the proposed venture is very appealing and well promoted, the founder can raise all of the required capital from outside investors and still retain control. However, most outside investors feel more comfortable if the founder is willing to risk his own money also. Offering stock to too many investors should be avoided, as that could constitute a public offering, which would have to be registered with the Securities and Exchange Commission.

Venture Capitalists

Another possible source of capital is from venture capital firms, who invest in high technology, fast growth companies. **They provide equity (risk) capital and loans to such companies with the idea of recouping their investment later by selling the company or by taking it public.** However, such largesse doesn't come without strings attached. To protect their interests, venture capitalists will often require a majority of the equity, or at least voting control, in exchange for their investment. If the founder isn't careful, he might find himself ending up with precious little equity in his brainchild.

The Author's Own Experience

When I started my business, I chose to form an S Corporation and seek investors. Although, in retrospect, I could have financed the initial capital (just barely), I decided to spread the risk and take in outside investors. As I had no exciting product idea or patent, I decided not to ask for founder's equity. Accordingly, the other investors and I invested on equal terms at one dollar per share for each share issued by the corporation. I managed to raise enough personal funds to ensure that I obtained 52% of the shares. As it turned out, the initial capital was exhausted before the company was well established. I was very fortunate that all the investors came up with the necessary additional capital and that I was able to maintain my 52% equity. Once the company became viable, we were able to finance working capital requirements with bank loans.

Chapter 6:

Running Lean and Mean

Minimizing Overhead

Now that the business has been capitalized and the money is in the bank, one must be very careful not to spend it all before the business gets off the ground. **Remember, if the initial capital is exhausted and more is needed, it is more difficult the second time around.** Here are a few suggestions on how to conserve capital.

Keep staffing to an absolute minimum.

Employees, with their wages, payroll taxes and fringe benefits, are the primary money drain in any company. Before hiring employees to do what you can't do yourself, investigate the possibility of subcontracting the tasks. Things like industrial design, accounting and payroll are best done by highly skilled outside services anyway.

Except for retail businesses, one should strive to hold down the cost of the business location.

It is not necessary for a manufacturer or a non-retail service business to have fancy quarters in a high rent district. In any case, the quarters should be rented and not bought. **Buying a store or place of business is a quick way to deplete capital.** Also, avoid the temptation to engage overly large quarters with the reasoning that there will be plenty of room to expand. Some expansion room should be provided for, of course, but committing to enough space for many years of growth is not the best use of money. Following the example of the crab—which sheds its shell and grows a bigger one when needed—is usually the more sensible approach.

Keep clear of big accounting firms.

For outside accounting and tax work, a start-up business should engage an independent CPA or a small accounting firm. The large national accounting firms should be avoided in the beginning, as their fees can be really staggering.

Avoid fancy law firms.

Do not put yourself in the hands of a major law firm, especially in the beginning. The legal work to set up the company and to make all the necessary filings can be done just as well by a smaller, less expensive independent lawyer or law firm. (If a large law firm were engaged by a small start-up for the initial legal work, a junior lawyer would probably be assigned anyway, but the fees would be higher than with a small firm.) High powered lawyers may eventually be needed for more complex tasks, such as litigation, labor relations, etc., but none of these apply with a start-up.

Avoid the "big shot" syndrome.

All too often the founder of a small business, having raised a pot of money to capitalize it, will spend it freely on the trappings of a big shot captain of industry, including fancy digs, a glamorous receptionist, company cars and—God forbid—a company airplane.

The Author's Own Experience

I once had the opportunity to invest in a start-up company founded by a couple of bright young engineers, who were previously employed by a major electronics firm. They had a very exciting product idea, and although I declined to invest, they were able to find a wealthy individual to back them. Once the seed money was in the bank and at their disposal, they went a little crazy. Right off the bat, they engaged a swanky suite of offices in a high priced office park, bought expensive company cars and leased a two engine aircraft, with the rationale that it would provide fast transportation to their customers. As neither of the principals could fly, they hired a full time pilot, who was assigned the position of sales manager! Needless to say, they ran through the initial capital in no time at all. Their mortified backer decided to cut his losses and refused to come up with more money. The company went bust, and the two bright young engineers went to work for another electronics concern. Although this example is rather extreme, it shows how fast the initial capital can be depleted by a start-up if spending is not closely watched.

Internet resources for small businesses:

- Download business forms at:
  http://.quicken.excite.com/small_business/cch/tools/contents

- "The Ultimate Business Connection":
  www.industry.net

- *Inc.* Magazine: www.inc.com

- "Start Up Wisdom": www.smalloffice.com/govt

- *New York Times*: www.nytimes.com

- *The Wall Street Journal*: www.wsj.com

- *USA Today*: www.usatoday.com

- *Entrepreneurial Edge* magazine: www.edgeonline.com

- *Barron's* Online: www.barrons.com

- "The Proven Path to Capital": www.moneyhunter.com

- "A World of Resources for Entrepreneurs": www.entreworld.org

- Federal Express: www.fedex.com

- United Parcel Service: www.ups.com

Chapter 7:

Keeping the Books

It's Not as Daunting as It Seems

Knowing exactly where the business stands at any given time is crucial. To accomplish this it is necessary to keep accurate financial books and generate periodic financial statements. **The trick is to keep it from getting too complicated.** Many entrepreneurs who may be well accomplished in the other aspects of business are overcome with anxiety when it comes to bookkeeping. They will often decide right away that they need to hire a financial controller, or at least a full charge bookkeeper. This is usually not necessary for a small start-up company. Instead, one can farm out many bookkeeping functions to outside accounting services, who make use of check copies, deposit slips, invoice copies and accounts payable to crank out financial statements each month. In addition, such services can be employed to calculate the payroll, generate payroll checks and prepare quarterly payroll tax reports. There are many accounting service firms to choose from, and their fees are very reasonable. In fact, many larger firms employ such services to reduce costs and to maintain confidentiality of payroll information.

The Checkbook Tells All

The most basic bookkeeping tool is the checkbook. Except for petty cash transactions, all expenditures should be made by writing checks and recording the nature of the expenditures in the check record. Likewise, all deposits to the bank account should be recorded on deposit slips, and the source of the funds should be noted. The accounting task is made easier if each check is coded to denote the classification of the expenditure.

For instance, capital expenditures could be coded in the 100 series:

101 ....furniture
102 ....machine tools
103 ....computer equipment
etc.

Expense items could be coded in the 200 series:

201.................................office salaries
202..utilities
203...rent
etc.

The checkbook is the most basic and important element of bookkeeping. All financial transactions
in a business finally come down to writing a check or
making a deposit. After all, the checkbook is the ultimate record of the flow of money in and out of the
business.

Small service businesses and product companies typically use cash
accounting. Cash accounting records when money comes in and when
the bills are paid.

Companies with inventory often use the accrual method of accounting.
Accrual accounting tracks when income is earned (independent of when
payment is received) and when expenses are incurred (not when the
bills are paid).

The Balance Sheet

A listing of the assets and liabilities of a business is called the Balance Sheet. Assets include such things as cash, inventory, accounts receivable and fixed assets (furniture, fixtures and other capital assets). Liabilities include accounts payable, borrowings and other debts. The difference between assets and liabilities is the net worth, or book value, of the business. Accordingly, as shown in Figure 2, total assets equal (or balance) the sum of liabilities and net worth. If the net worth is a positive number, the business is solvent; if it is negative, the business is insolvent. **The balance sheet shows the current financial strength of the business on a given date and doesn't speak to its current profitability, which is another matter.**

Figure 2

Example Balance Sheet
at December 31

Assets

Cash	$10,000
Accounts Receivable	120,000
Inventory	100,000
Fixed Assets	75,000
Total Assets	$305,000

Liabilities

Accounts Payable	$100,000
Accrued Wages	25,000
Bank Debts	50,000
Total Liabilities	$175,000

Net Worth

Net Worth	130,000
	$305,000

The Profit and Loss (P&L) Statement

The P&L statement, also called Earnings Statement, reveals whether a business is currently making or losing money in its operations. When sales revenues in a given period are compared with the associated costs and expenses, the difference is the profit or loss in the business for that period. A typical P&L statement is shown in Figure 3. In this example, sales revenues include the total sales value of the goods shipped and invoiced in the stated period. The Cost of Goods Sold (COGS) includes those costs that were directly involved with the sales, such as the material that went into the goods and the labor required to produce the goods. The difference between the sales revenues and COGS is the Gross Profit. Expenses include all other costs not directly tied to the production of the goods sold, such as management salaries, office expenses, rent, utilities, insurance, etc. What is left is the profit, or loss, as the case may be. In this example, the income tax due on the profit is not shown.

Neither the balance sheet nor the P&L statement, taken alone, reveal the whole financial story
about a business. In fact, many fast growth but undercapitalized businesses may show booming profits but
weak balance sheets, due mainly to excessive bank debt.
Conversely, a financially strong but moribund company
may have an impressive balance sheet but little or no
profits.

Figure 3

Example Profit & Loss Statement
Month Ending June 30

Sales Revenues	$ 65,000

Cost of Goods Sold:

Materials	20,000
Labor	10,000
Gross Profit	$ 35,000

Expenses:

Office Salaries	10,000
Rent	1,500
Utilities	1,000
Telephone	2,000
Insurance	1,000
Miscellaneous	10,000
Total Expenses	$ 25,500

Operating Profit	$ 9,500

Other Accounting Tasks

Besides the checkbook and financial statements, other accounting tasks include:

• an accounts payable schedule, listing all amounts owed to others and for what,
• an accounts receivable schedule, listing all amounts owed to the business, by whom and for what,
• payroll records and quarterly withholding tax returns,
• federal and state unemployment insurance records,
• franchise tax returns (corporations only),
• property tax returns and records,
• state sales tax returns and records,
• income tax returns,
• casualty and liability insurance records,
• group health insurance records, if applicable.

Many of these tasks can be performed by outside services at very reasonable rates. Even when the company has grown to the point of engaging a full time financial person, some of the tasks listed above are better done outside, especially payroll administration.

Chapter 8:

Financial Controls

Why Financial Controls?

Financial controls in a small business are no less important than in a large one. Without financial controls, unwarranted expenditures can mushroom, even if the intentions are good. On the dark side, the lack of financial controls leaves the business open to questionable practices or, worse, embezzelement. In a small business one person may be handling all the accounting functions, and if that person feels under-paid, the temptation to skim the till might become overpowering.

Checkbook Protocol

• One cardinal rule to follow is to ensure that the person who keeps the checkbook is not the same one who reconciles the bank statement. If this rule is followed, irregularities (such as unauthorized checks or forgery) will almost certainly be detected.

• Keep check signatories to a minimum. While it makes sense to have more than one authorized signature—in case the primary signatory is indisposed and unable to sign a check—the number of people who can sign should be limited. A common practice is to require that two or more alternate signatories sign checks in the absence of the chief executive.

• Set a maximum amount on checks that alternate signatories can sign.

• Require that a voucher, indicating what the payment is for, accompany each check submitted for signature. This is helpful for the signatory as well as for the payee. A copy of the suppliers invoice, or invoices, should be attached and should be reviewed by the check signer.

Purchasing

• Establish a policy that requires the approval of certain expenditures, especially capital outlays, such as expensive machinery and office equipment.

• Require that all bills be verified before being presented for payment. For instance, a supplier's invoice should be compared with the corresponding purchase order and with the packing list accompanying the goods received.

• Require that the receipt of purchased material be recorded by a person different from the one who ordered the material. A scam played by crooked purchasing agents is to issue a purchase order to a bogus supplier and then generate a corresponding bogus invoice, which he or she then approves for payment.

The Author's Own Experience

For a number of years the in-house accounting functions at my company were handled by an executive secretary who was also a full charge bookkeeper. She was very capable and hardworking. Contrary to the guidelines outlined above, she maintained the checkbook and also reconciled the bank statements. When she failed to return from a short vacation, I discovered that she had forged my signature to a check that she wrote to herself in the amount of $5,000. An investigation revealed that she had been pocketing cash receipts and dipping into the petty cash fund. In all, this employee embezzled over $10,000. Better financial controls might have prevented this unfortunate situation. The police were of no real help. However, she had fled to another state while still owing General Motors Acceptance Corporation for her car. In a few weeks GMAC ran her down, repossessed the car, and informed me of her whereabouts. She finally made full restitution under administration by the court, and we ended up losing only the interest on our stolen money. We were lucky that the loss was as small as it was, for the record is full of companies that were ruined by embezzlement.

Chapter 9:

Managing Cash

Cash Has Wings!

It's amazing how quickly cash can disappear. When a business is doing poorly, operating expenses can deplete cash rapidly. At the other extreme, when business is expanding—especially in manufacturing or distribution—cash is rapidly used up. The reason for this is that cash has to be spent to purchase materials and labor in advance of when the resulting products can be shipped and the money collected. **Paradoxically then, a small business can run out of cash quickly when business is good, and unless it can raise additional cash quickly, the business could find itself in a severe financial crisis.** Some guidelines for conserving cash, or raising additional cash, follow.

Be Careful with Credit

Be careful about offering credit terms to new customers. Unless you are selling to a blue chip company or to someone with a good credit rating, don't hesitate to ask for cash before shipment or cash on delivery (COD). For special, non-standard products or services one should ask for full or partial advance payment with the order.

When selling to a foreign customer, the best practice is to require payment by letter of credit, whereby the customer establishes credit at its bank (preferably a U.S. bank) in favor of the seller, for the purpose of ensuring payment when the goods are shipped. The bank releases the funds to the seller upon the presentation of shipping documents.

Collecting Receivables

Hopefully, with good accounting methods and prudent policies regarding credit, overdue accounts receivables will be kept to a minimum. Even customers with okay credit ratings are sometimes slow to pay, and this is especially true if no pressure is applied. **Don't let a receivable get long overdue before applying pressure.** As soon as a receivable has passed the 45-day mark (or the time period appropriate to your business), a reminder should be sent by fax, telephone or e-mail. Relentlessly follow up on a regular basis with increasingly stronger language until the entire amount is collected. When there are many overdue accounts, this can be a time consuming job. However, the task can be made easier by maintaining an up-to-date accounts receivable listing arranged by age. In this way the overdue accounts will show up clearly. (In extreme cases a collection agency can be employed, but they will take a large slice of whatever is collected.) It is also important that the right hand knows what the left hand is doing in your business: don't ship new orders or provide additional services to delinquent clients until their account is brought up-to-date.

Cash Management Hints

• One way to conserve cash is to delay payment of bills as long as possible without hurting one's credit rating. A supplier's invoice with net 30 days payment terms can ordinarily be paid in 45 days without causing a stir. However, one must be careful in playing this game, for an irate supplier might react to slow payment by shipping C.O.D. in the future.

• Another way to raise cash quickly is to sell accounts receivable to a **factor**, which is a type of finance company that purchases accounts receivable and handles the collection, but at a steep discount. This source of funds should be used only if a bank loan is not available and the situation is desperate.

• While a mature company may find it more economical to buy capital equipment rather than leasing it, a cash strapped small company will usually be better advised to lease in order to conserve cash.

Bank Loans

• When additional working capital is needed, the best place to get it is at the bank. **That is why it is essential to establish a close relationship with a bank early on.** This should begin when the checking account is opened, and developed through ongoing contact. Don't wait until you need to borrow the money. Invite your account executive to visit and become acquainted with your business.

• Do not always make your deposits at the bank's drive-through. Take the time to go inside the office where you set-up your account, make your deposit in person, and greet your banker. Tell him or her the positive news about your business. By doing this you will find it easier should you ever need to ask for a loan.

• Prepare in advance: Ask your banker to establish a line of credit at an agreed rate of interest, so that when you need additional cash to get through a rough spot, it can be drawn without delay.

Cash Forecasting

An entrepreneur's nightmare is to wake up one morning and discover that there isn't enough cash to meet the payroll. This dismal scenario can be avoided by keeping a current cash forecast. **This is nothing more than listing expected cash income and cash outflows for the next few months.** A typical cash forecast is shown in Figure 4. In this example a capital expenditure in month #2 would overdraw the account if not for the bank loan made that month. Forecasting allows time to arrange the bank loan in an orderly manner and meet the payroll without a panic call to the bank in the last minute.

Figure 4

Example Cash Forecast

	Month #1	Month #2	Month #3
Beginning Balance	$10,500	$ 19,000	$13,500
Incoming Cash:			
Accounts Receivable	62,000	50,000	60,000
Misc. Income	1,000	1,000	1,000
Bank Loan	-0-	50,000	-0-
Total Available	$73,500	$120,000	$74,500
Expenditures:			
Salaries & Wages	13,000	13,000	13,000
Rent	1,500	1,500	1,500
Utilities	1,000	1,000	1,000
Taxes	1,000	1,000	1,000
Insurance	2,000	2,000	2,000
Inventory	24,000	25,000	24,000
Miscellaneous	12,000	13,000	12,000
Capital Equipment	-0-	50,000	-0-
Total	$54,500	$106,500	$54,500
Ending Balance	$19,000	$ 13,500	$20,000

When All Else Fails

Sometimes, especially when a business is rapidly growing, a company may find that despite all its cash conservation efforts, it must borrow more and more from its bank. A point may be reached where the interest expense severely erodes profits, and the debt on the balance sheet begins to look lopsided. The business may then decide to seek equity financing to pay off at least some of the debt. This is normally accomplished by the sale of additional stock in the company. (See Chapter 5). It must be recognized, however, that raising capital in this way dilutes the equity of the existing owners—unless the owners are prepared to invest more also.

Businesses based on high growth industry have an advantage in arranging equity loans. However, the overall economic outlook for businesses throughout the U.S. is a factor investors keep in mind. For current business trends see: *The Survey of Current Business* published by the Department of Commerce (801) 524-5116.

Important Tips to Remember
When Approaching Potential Investors:

• Show sound business management practices. (If you are not sure what this involves, then contact your local SCORE office and arrange to meet with a counselor.) You don't need to re-invent the wheel—but you do need to know how to use it. There is a science and an art to managing a business successfully, and investors will want assurance that you are qualified.

• Represent your business accurately. Don't embellish projected revenue figures. Don't try to impress investors with fancy (expensive) offices or the other trappings of success—they will want to know that you will use each dollar wisely.

• Determine exactly what your product or services is and who your market is. (See the section on Business Plans.) Then, clearly explain this "what" and "who" in written form. If writing is not one of your strengths, hire someone to help you, or enlist the input of someone with business experience (such as the SCORE volunteer). Investors cannot develop confidence in a business that is not clearly explained. After all, if you can't explain it to them quickly, how will you explain it to potential customers?

• Figure your capital expenses and monthly business expenses will be greater than anticipated. Estimate your sales will be less than you hope.

Taxes Pertaining to Businesses:

Federal:
Employee Payroll Tax
Social Security Tax
Excise Tax
Owner's and/or Corporation's Income Tax
Unemployment Tax

State:
Unemployment Tax
Income Tax
Sales Tax
Franchise Tax

Local:
Sales Tax
Real Estate Taxes
Personal Property Taxes
Licenses

Chapter 10:

Insurance—
A Necessary
Burden

Choose Insurance Carefully

Nowadays, businesses large and small find that insurance against a host of risks is necessary to avoid a severe financial setback. **Whereas some major corporations find it more practical to self insure against certain risks, a small business must buy insurance against a major loss or risk bankruptcy.** The total cost of insurance stands out as a major expense item for any business. For this reason it is very important to shop the insurance market and avoid overlapping or excessive coverage. Some of the various types of insurance that a business might purchase are discussed in this chapter.

Information on the Internet regarding insurance:
* Guide to Small Business Insurance: www.iiaa.iix.com/smallbiz.html
* Insurance Information Institute: www.iii.org

Casualty and Fire Insurance

Insurance underwriters classify various business pursuits in terms of risk. Obviously, a fireworks manufacturer represents a greater fire risk than a hardware store. **Accordingly, one should be certain that the insurance company is not wrongly classifying one's business in a higher risk category than is justified.** Another point to consider is the deductible amount in the policy. In general, a good rule is to set the deductible amount as high as can be managed, since by doing so the premium can be reduced substantially.

Keep in a separate location a complete inventory of your business property, noting quantity and costs. (A video or photographs may be helpful.)

Note: It is possible to be held responsible for the loss of others' (clients') property located at your place of business. Ask your insurance provider about Fire Legal Liability Insurance or obtain a signed waiver from the person or business that owns the property.

General Liability Insurance

Unfortunately, we live in an era of rampant litigation. People file lawsuits against others over the most trivial matters. This dismal situation is compelling businesses to build their defenses by taking out substantial amounts of liability insurance. Unlike property risk insurance, where the maximum loss is limited to the value of the property, there is hardly a limit to what someone can sue for and sometimes get awarded by a jury. Even multi-billion dollar corporations have been driven into bankruptcy by class action lawsuits. There is no rule of thumb for setting the amount of liability coverage. So much depends on the type of business and how much exposure it has to possible lawsuits. Obviously a trampoline manufacturer is at greater risk of being sued than a stationary store. **One is best advised to take out as much coverage as the business can comfortably afford.** Fortunately, the premium rate for liability insurance decreases as the liability limit increases.

Workers' Compensation Insurance

Employers are well advised to obtain Workers' Compensation Insurance, which is regulated by the state and covers medical expenses related to on-the-job claims for injury. It also makes payments to workers while they are temporarily or permanently disabled. **The insurance premiums are paid by the employer for the benefit of its employees.** In exchange, the employer usually is indemnified against any legal claims by an injured or disabled employee.

Insurance for Businesses:
Fire, Liability, Automotive, Workers' Compensation, Business Interruption, Burglary Insurance, Glass Insurance, Rent Insurance, Group Life Insurance, Group Health Insurance, Disability Insurance, Key-Man Insurance

Group Health Insurance

Of all the employee benefits that can be sponsored by an employer, group health insurance stands out as the most important. In fact, nowadays most employees, with the possible exception of migrants or itinerant workers, expect it as their right. **With medical and hospital costs what they are, an employer would be hard pressed to find good workers without a competitive health insurance benefit plan to offer.** The cost of a group health insurance plan depends on many things, the most significant of which are listed below.

• An HMO (Health Maintenance Organization) and other managed care plans are more restrictive but less costly than more conventional health plans that allow the patient to choose his or her own health care providers.

• The cost increases when the coverage includes such things as pregnancy, psychiatric care, dentistry and drug prescriptions.

• Most group health plans provide for a yearly deductible (the amount of health costs paid by the employee before the insurance coverage kicks in) and a stipulated co-payment (the fraction of the balance paid by the employee). **The larger the deductible and co-payments the lower the premium.**

Once the structure of the health plan as been selected, it remains to decide the split in the premiums between the employer and employee. At this writing, group insurance plans are in private hands; therefore, there is no law governing how the premium payment must be shared. **In general, however, the employee is expected to pay at least part of the premium.** For example, it is common practice for the employer to pay the full premium for the employee's coverage, and the employee pays for his or her dependents' coverage. Many other premium splits are possible.

The Author's Own Experience

Believing insurance should be designed to protect against catastrophic loss only and not against small losses, we opted for large deductibles in the fire and casualty policies. Likewise, the group health insurance incorporated a reasonably high deductible, and the co-payment was set at 30% up to $5,000.00, with the plan then paying 100% of hospital costs. The limit of hospital coverage was set high (at $1,000,000) to protect against a catastrophic illness. In so doing, we were able to reduce insurance premiums and lighten the financial burden on employees who were insuring their dependents.

Chapter 11:

Marketing

Nothing Happens Until Something is Sold

A popular saying goes, "Nothing happens in business until something is sold." And nothing *will* be sold until the market knows about the product or service offered. The market, whether local or international, is surprisingly difficult to reach, inform and convince. **The task of reaching potential customers, informing them of the merits of the product or service and convincing them to buy yours instead of theirs, is called marketing.** This is a major expense for most companies, old or new. For this reason a start-up company is well advised to ensure that it gets the most bang for the buck. Whether the business is introducing a product or a service, the first priority is to reach and inform the marketplace.

The very best, and most believable, publicity is by word-of-mouth. For a retail business, it may be the only thing required to reach potential customers, especially if the market is restricted to a local area. However, if the business seeks nationwide or international markets, word-of-mouth publicity alone won't be enough, and other measures must be employed.

Publicity

Most trade magazines have a section entitled "New Products," where photographs and captions describe recently released products or services. **However, as new product editors are usually swamped with submittals, it is important that the photograph (preferably color) and write-up are especially interesting and appealing.** There is no charge for a new product release, and since it has an editorial image, it is sometimes more credible to the reader than a paid-for display ad. The drawback is that a new product release is a one time only opportunity, usually featured only once in a particular magazine. Another source of free publicity is the business section of the local newspaper. Here again, the news release must be well presented to catch the interest of the business editor.

Publicity is free "advertising" (such as press releases) that occurs when the media relates news about your business based on information you've submitted, but not under your control.

Advertising

If the market for the product or service is spread out over a large area, or even the world, advertising is an effective way to reach it. Advertising is expensive, so great care must be exercised in designing the ad and choosing the advertising medium. This is best done by an advertising agency. Not any advertising agency, but one that has experience in the same or similar fields. Close coordination with the agency is necessary for good results. The agency can also help in choosing the media in which to advertise. It should be noted, however, that ad agencies earn a commission on each ad placed, so they tend to recommend high advertising budgets to their clients.

Promotion includes: advertising, speeches, special events, direct mail, newsletters, brochures, on-hold tapes, premiums—all marketing activities where the business being promoted controls the message.

Representatives and Agents

Only larger, well established companies can afford to maintain sales offices across the country or across the world. Smaller companies, even those with nationwide or worldwide markets, often use independent representatives or agents instead. Representatives, who sell in the domestic market, cover a particular area and are paid a commission on the value of the orders that they obtain for their principals. Foreign agents, on the other hand, usually import products from their principals and then resell them in local currency. **Choosing representatives and agents who are knowledgeable in the particular field and who are well connected in the marketplace is extremely important.** A bad choice will waste a lot of money and time. It is worthwhile to network the search with as many sources of information as time will allow. One approach is to seek recommendations from other businesses in the same general field, but who are not competitors.

Trade publications and associations may be able to direct you to appropriate representatives and agents for your business.

In-House Salesmen

As the business grows, it may become increasingly difficult for the founder to properly handle the marketing functions along with all the other duties. (Remembering that "nothing happens until something is sold," it's important that sales always be given top priority.) The founder then realizes that one or more sales people will have to be hired. Finding the right person is a real challenge.

In a small business the temptation is to save money and hire a green but inexpensive person for the job. Quite the contrary! A start-up business cannot afford the time it takes to train and evaluate the effectiveness of an inexperienced salesman. **What is needed is a person who has experience and a proven track record with your product or service, or at least in the same field of interest.** Such a person may cost more but will be worth the extra expense. Besides experience, the candidate should have a pleasing personality, a sincere manner, ambition, and a command of the language, both in speech and in writing.

Important Tips for a Positive Business Image:

- Network with compatible businesses. If you'll refer people whose needs are outside your services, they will reciprocate.

- Develop a slogan or motto that exemplifies your business, then print it on all marketing materials. A logo may be important also. Consistency and repetition are the keys tocreating a memorable visual presence.

- Surprise your clients with more than they expect.

- Ensure your phone system is caller-friendly, and, whenever possible, first answered by a person, not a machine.

- Publish a client newsletter.

- Help your clients by giving them information they need, before they even know they need it.

- Thank and reward anyone (internally and outside the company) who refers new customers to you.

- Send out press releases on a regular basis.

- Conduct customer surveys.

The Author's Own Experience

When I got around to hiring a salesman, I made the mistake of looking for a bargain. When he didn't work out, I promoted an insider who really wasn't qualified. In each case it took months or years to finally realize that these employees were not going to enable my company to meet the goals we had set. We finally got smart and employed a person with experience selling in our field. From that point on sales grew at a much faster pace. Later on we hired another experienced salesman, at which point we felt justified in hiring and training green salesmen as the Sales Department expanded.

Chapter 12:

Company Policies

Establish Policies Before Hiring

Before the first person is hired and put on the payroll, a set of written company policies should already be in place. Without written policies, the boss will be constantly peppered with awkward requests and clarifications. **Before preparing a list of policies, the employer should become acquainted with the federal and state labor laws and workplace safety regulations, as well as any city ordinances that may apply.** As a minimum, the published policies should address and define the following points:

• **Employee Classifications**—defining hourly, salaried, full time and part time employees.

• **Working Hours**—defining regular working hours for hourly and salaried employees.

• **Overtime Pay**—defining overtime hours and the overtime wage rate.

• **Pay Periods**—for hourly employees (usually biweekly) and salaried employees (usually semimonthly).

• **Paid Holidays**—posted at the beginning of each year.

• **Paid Vacation**—the rules stating the number of paid vacation days after a year (or a minimum number of hours) as a full time employee; the number of vacation days earned after X years of service; the rule regarding pay in lieu of vacation; and the policy regarding accrued vacation pay on termination of employment.

• **Travel Compensation**—the rule stating how an hourly employee is paid for time spent traveling and working on company business.

• **Leave of Absence**—the policy regarding paid or unpaid absence for medical leave, jury duty, funeral leave, pregnancy, military service or for other reasons; and the policy regarding resumption of service accrual and benefits after a break in employment.

• **Wage Reviews**—the policy stating the criteria for wage increases and the frequency of reviews.

• **Termination**—rules covering notice of termination or pay in lieu thereof and the policy regarding accrued vacation pay on termination with cause.

• **Grievances**—the rule stating the method for submiting a grievance and the recourse available if no action is taken.

• **Computers and Software**—the rules restricting use of computers for company business and prohibiting loading of personal software.

• **Employer/Employee Relations**—the policies and rules covering equal employment opportunity and sexual harassment.

Policies regarding working hours, overtime pay and hourly/salaried classifications are subject to regulations issued by the U.S. Department of Labor, which should be consulted for the latest rules. At this writing, the law requires that an hourly employee be paid only for the hours worked and does not require pay for jury duty, sick leave or other absences.

Loans to Employees

Unless the policy is clear, the day will inevitably come when an employee will approach the boss for an advance on his or her paycheck to meet a financial emergency of some kind. The request may even be for a more substantial loan to be paid back by payroll check deductions over a period of time. Once this sort of thing starts, there is no end to it. Other employees find out, and before long the company finds itself in the banking business. **The best way out of this awkward situation is to introduce the workforce to an existing credit union, and let it take over the banking function.** The employer can cooperate by arranging automatic payroll deductions for deposit in the credit union.

Company Cars

The best policy regarding company cars is not to have any—company cars that is. Nothing creates more management headaches than how to deal with company owned or leased cars. Those who are granted cars are envied or resented by those who aren't, and unless all the cars are exactly the same make, jealousies and resentments can arise among those who have them. Furthermore, the IRS now requires that personal usage of a company car must be reported as additional remuneration for the employee, and that can become another headache. **The simple and fair solution to the problem is to establish a policy for reimbursing employees for the use of their personal cars for company business.** To make matters easier, the Internal Revenue Service conveniently publishes a guideline mileage rate, which can be used as the basis for reimbursement.

Corporate Credit Cards

Corporate credit cards can also create awkward situations. Unless the credit card is scrupulously used only for company business, the employee is faced with separating personal charges from business charges when submitting an expense report. For instance, most large hotels offer a number of services that can be charged to the room—such as bars, spas, nightclubs, tours and theater tickets—all of which appear on the same bill at the end of the stay. If the hotel bill is charged on a corporate credit card, the employee must then reimburse the company for any personal charges incurred. **It is much better to require that the employee charge business expenses on a personal credit card and then obtain reimbursement for business expenses from the company.** If substantial charges are anticipated, as during a long sales trip abroad, cash can be advanced to the salesman beforehand and then deducted from the trip expenses reported.

Chapter 13:

Employee Pensions

Defined Benefit Plan

The most common type of pension plan is one with defined benefits, which means that the company's periodic contribution to each participant's account is a set amount and is independent of how profitable the company may or may not be. This type of pension plan also allows employees to contribute to their accounts as well. A popular type of defined benefits pension plan is one that complies with Section 401(k) of the Internal Revenue Code. Such a qualified plan allows the employer to treat its contributions as deductible expenses. By the same token, the employee can defer the tax on the company contributions and on the total accumulated earnings in his or her account until the money is paid out at retirement or at termination of employment.

Profit Sharing Plan

Unlike a defined benefit plan, a profit sharing plan provides that the employer will contribute a
fraction of its before-tax-profit each year to a profit
sharing fund, the financial interest in which is shared
by the plan participants. An employee becomes a plan
participant after a specified length of service (such as
one year). The fraction of the company's annual contribution that goes into a participant's account is typically
equal to the ratio of the participant's annual remuneration to the total annual remuneration of all participants.
Each participant's vested interest in their account
increases yearly by a set formula. In this type of pension
plan all contributions are paid in by the employer and
none by the participant. Here again, if the plan complies
with the requirements of the Internal Revenue Code,
the contributions and earnings in the fund are tax free
to the participants until the money is paid out at retirement or at termination of employment.

Writing a Pension Plan

Writing a pension plan that complies with the IRS and with ERISA (Employee Retirement Income Security Act) is a daunting task and should be done by a professional. Such things as eligibility, length of service, breaks in service, vesting and other stipulations must be properly defined in any qualifying plan. A lawyer specializing in this field can be hired to write the plan. Or, one can take advantage of the prototype plans offered as a service by investment brokerage firms in exchange for their being assigned to handle the investments of the pension fund. Since the pension fund investments are better handled by a third party professional anyway, making use of the brokerage firm's service to prepare the plan makes a lot of sense. Furthermore, the IRS and ERISA requirements are subject to change from time to time, and the brokerage firm can usually be relied upon to keep its prototype plans current with the law.

Chapter 14:

Why Not Buy
a Going Business?

The previous pages have dealt with the risks and pitfalls associated with starting a business from scratch. Another option is to buy a going business that fits the buyer's field of interest. Buying a going business offers the obvious advantage that the business has weathered the critical, and often fatal, first few years of infancy. It also saves a lot of time.

Questions and Answers

Buying a business is not without risk, since the buyer may be unaware of certain shortcomings and potential liabilities that may exist. Some questions that must be answered are:

• Why does the present owner want to sell? Does he really want to retire at age 50 and travel, or does he know that his product or service has fallen behind the competition, and he has neither the energy nor resources to catch up?

• Do the financial statements reflect the true health of the company? How much of the inventory is stale and unsalable? Are the other assets fairly valued?

• What about undisclosed liabilities? Are there present or pending lawsuits against the company?

• If the land and building are part of the deal, are they in compliance with local and federal codes? Keep in mind that the present owner may be permitted to be in violation of certain codes or regulations under a grandfather clause, but any new owner will have to be in full compliance. Removal of asbestos insulation and cleaning up soil contamination can be real nightmares.

• Are there growth prospects for the business? One certainly doesn't want to pay a premium for a business that has stagnated because of new competition or obsolescence.

• Can new management improve the profitability of the business? Very often older companies have allowed themselves to become overstaffed with expensive overhead employees, whose salaries have increased with seniority beyond the market wage for similar skills. Are there people employed for tasks that could be more economically contracted to outside services?

• Will the absence of the present owner seriously debilitate the business? If so, can he be persuaded to phase out gradually and pass on his expertise and customer contacts?

Chapter 15:

How Much is the Business Worth?

Whether buying or selling a business, the question as to how much it is worth can be extremely vexing. In the first place, the present owner (especially if he is the founder) may have a strong emotional attachment to the business and will tend to overstate its worth. The buyer, on the other hand, is looking to pay the lowest possible dollar. The trick is to find the price that a reasonable buyer would pay and that a reasonable seller would accept for the business. Various methods are used to put a value on a business. Some of these are discussed in the following pages.

Multiple of Book Value

This method applies mainly to businesses whose book value (assets minus liabilities) is made up mostly of inventory and fixed assets (machinery, equipment and fixtures). Such businesses would include retail stores, heavy manufacturers and transportation companies. These types of businesses may be valued at more or less than book value, depending on the earnings record of the business. If the company is losing money, it may actually be valued at less than book value. Keep in mind that the actual liquidation value of the fixed assets of a business may be less than the value on the books (cost less accumulated depreciation), and unless old or obsolete items have been written off the books, the value of the inventory could be over stated. These are good reasons why an outside accounting firm should be employed to audit the books prior to closing a deal.

Multiple of Earnings

For less capital intensive businesses, the more favored method is to reach **a valuation based more on the earnings record of the business and less on its book value.** Such businesses would include light manufacturers and services. If the business is static or slowly growing, an investor might pay five to ten times the after tax earnings, calculating that his investment will be returned in five or ten years (compared with twenty years if he puts his money into a safe U.S. Treasury bond paying 5% interest). At the other extreme, a glamorous, fast growth business in a bull market can reach values that exceed 30, 40 or 50 times earnings, based on the expectation that the earnings of the business will rapidly increase in future years.

Blue Sky

What is the value of a company that has never made a profit and has a zero or negative book value? The quick answer, using the above valuation methods, is that the company is worthless. **Not necessarily!** In fact, many young companies in exciting new fields, but which have never made a profit, are able to raise large sums of money in the stock market solely on the "blue sky" promise of a bonanza to come. For such companies the belief within the stock market is that the future profits will soon wipe out the present deficit, and a dollar invested now will be worth many more in just a few years. The point is that the methods used to value a mature company—values based on book value or earnings—cannot be used to value a new start-up. **Instead, a start-up business must be valued on the basis of the idea behind it and the reputation of its management.**

The Author's Own Experience

In the early years of my company we acquired a small start-up business that was being divested by its parent company. This small business had just developed a product that was attractive to us, but at that time there had been no sales. The assets of the business consisted of a small inventory, some production fixtures and test equipment. The goodwill of the business (the value in excess of the book value) consisted of the designs, manufacturing drawings, some market research and a supply of sales brochures. As the business had no sales or earnings record, it was difficult to evaluate the goodwill. We could only guess at how well the product would sell in the market place. We finally reached an agreement whereby we would pay cash for the hard assets at book value and pay for the goodwill by way of a 5% royalty on future sales, for a period of ten years. In this way we only had to pay for the goodwill in proportion to how well the business fared. In fact, the acquired business prospered from the very beginning, and after five years of growing royalty payments we negotiated a lump sum settlement with the seller to terminate the royalties.

Checklist

☐   Test your idea for acceptance in the marketplace.

☐   Identify competitors, their locations and their pricing.

☐   Form a business plan and prepare an operations forecast to determine the amount of capital required. Don't be undercapitalized.

☐   Choose the type of organization best suited to your planned business.

☐   Choose a business name that alludes to the product or service offered. Check for conflicts with existing business names.

☐   If you cannot raise the initial capital yourself, choose from the various means available to raise the money.

☐   Once the capital is raised, spend it wisely.

☐   Avoid employing people for tasks that can be done better and for less by outside services.

❏ Maintain a good set of financial books, but use out side accounting services as much as possible.

❏ Install financial controls to prevent excessive spend ing and embezzlement.

❏ Buy insurance to protect against catastrophic losses, but don't over insure. Design a group health plan to provide essential protection for minimum cost.

❏ Establish a marketing plan. Get the word out to the marketplace about your new product or service.

❏ Choose in-house sales people and outside representives very carefully.

❏ To avoid awkward policy decisions and disgruntled employees, set down the company poli cies before the first person is hired.

❏ Have you considered buying a going business instead of starting one from scratch? If so, make sure that the business is viable and that you pay a fair price.

Conclusion

The old proverb "Nothing ventured, nothing gained" is certainly true. Unless one is lucky enough to inherit a fortune, the only way to build one is to take risks. Starting a business is certainly risky, but the risks can be minimized if the entrepreneur has a good idea, a business plan, raises enough capital and runs the business adroitly. **There is hardly a better feeling than to have started and built a successful business, to have sensed the market recognition of its products or services and to have witnessed the growing prosperity of its employees.** All this leads to a wonderful feeling of accomplishment and to the conviction that it was all worth the risk.